Grey

Body Poems

Compiled by John Foster

Contents

D0321561

Acknowledgements

The Editor and Publisher wish to thank the following who have kindly given permission for the use of copyright material:

Paul Cookson for 'Why is a bottom called a bottom?' © 1995 Paul Cookson; Eric Finney for 'Elbows and knees' © 1995 Eric Finney; John Foster for 'Feet are for . . .', 'I am the boss', 'Your heart' and 'With my hand' all © 1995 John Foster; Jill Townsend for 'Legs' © 1995 Jill Townsend; Celia Warren for 'I fell over at playtime' © 1995 Celia Warren.

Feet are for...

Kicking up leaves and snow,
and for marching to and fro,
for running up and down hill,
and standing up straight and still.

Feet are for hopping and skipping,
for sliding and for slipping,
for splashing in puddles and rain,
and for jumping again and again.

John Foster

Legs

Centipedes have lots and lots.
Sheep and cows have four.
I have only two legs
and I don't need any more.

Jill Townsend

Elbows and knees

Knees and elbows.
Elbows and knees.
Your legs and your arms
Couldn't bend without these.

Eric Finney

I am the boss

I am the boss.
What I say goes.
Clap your hands
And touch your toes.

I am the boss.
Look over here.
Waggle your thumbs
And scratch your ear.

I am the boss.
Jump like a clown.
Bend your knees
And all sit down!

John Foster

Your heart

Thump! Thump!
Your heart is a pump.
It beats all night and day,
Pumping blood around you
While you sleep and while you play

Race around the playground.
Put your hand upon your vest.
Feel your heart beat faster
As it thumps inside your chest.

John Foster

I fell over at playtime

I fell over at playtime,
I got up and found
   one cut knee
   one bumped head
   a pair of muddy hands
   and
   a wobbly tooth.

I went home at hometime
And my mum found
   a plaster for my knee
   a hat for my head
   gloves for my hands
   and
   a nice big gap
   in my grin.

Celia Warren

With my hand

With my hand I can turn on a tap,
I can give you a clap,
I can scratch my nose,
I can tickle my toes.

With my hand I can scoop up sand,
I can hold your hand,
I can point to the sky,
I can wave goodbye!

John Foster

Why is a bottom called a bottom?

The bottom of your body
is the bit that's on the ground.
So why is a bottom called
   a bottom,
when it's only halfway down?

Paul Cookson